the MFA Monthly
NO.1

the MFA Monthly
VOLUME 1, NO. 1

April 2012

Editor   Chris Pappas

Fiction   Christopher Murphy

Poetry   Daniel Robbins

Essay   Sy Hoahwah

Cover Art   Rebecca Pappas

Layout   Chris Pappas

© 2012 by USPOCO BOOOKS

the MFA Monthly

NO. 1

VOLUME 1

the MFA Monthly

is produced and published by USPOCO BOOKS,
in partnership with
ManuFacturedArtists.com.

Submission & Subscription Info

Submissions are read year round. We only guarantee a response
if accepted. After three weeks, if you have not heard from our
staff, you may inquire via one email on the status of a submitted
work.

Send your original and unpublished work (three to nine pages
of poetry, one story or one essay) to uspocobooks@gmail.com.
Simultaneous submissions are fine, of course.

Send cover submissions of original art or photography as an image file of at least 300 DPI. Keep in mind that this a pocket-sized
magazine with dimensions of about 5 X 7 inches.

Include month, genre and author's name in the subject line.
Submissions may also be considered for publication @ Manu-
FacturedArtists.com, a blog of the arts.

Do not include contributor notes or bios, for we do not publish
them.

We only accept email submissions. Each contributor will receive
five free copies of the magazine. USPOCO BOOKS will ship
your contributor's copies to any five addresses in the continental
US. Additional copies may be purchased at Amazon.com, us-
poco.com or your local independent bookstore. Ask your local
bookstore to carry USPOCO magazines and books!

SUBSCRIBE NOW FOR ONLY $25 FOR THE FIRST YEAR
AND GET THE FIRST ISSUE SHIPPED IMMEDIATELY
AND FREE OF CHARGE: **USPOCOBOOKS@GMAIL.COM.**

the MFA Monthly

NO. 1

USPOCO BOOKS
Pheonix, AZ

Christopher Murphy

My Dog in Heat

I woke up one morning and my dog's vagina was near my face. It was swollen and pink, like a kid's eye with bad conjunctivitis, and it smelled thick. While babysitting two nights previous, my little sister had dragged her teddy bear across the floor and my dog began to hump it. My dog hunched over the bear and thrust back against one of its arms. My little sister cried and tried to pull her bear away. This only made my dog hump faster. My dog, Tam, which was short for Tam O' Shanter, had the guilty look of a public nose picker.

My dog was many things—a digger, a chewer, a urinator whenever strangers came to the house. She had a lip that permanently curled above her left canine, which my father called her 'Elvis lip'. Like most things of pure and royal blood, she was retarded from inbreeding. People would call her 'handsome' until they attempted to pet her and she peed on their feet. But she had never been a humper.

At breakfast, my father had pulled up his pant leg to adjust his sock, and Tam began to hump his foot. Her back was curved, and she rubbed her puffy vagina on his shin and the back of his hand. My father picked her up, humping the air now, and investigated her nethers.

"Alex," he said. "Have you seen this?" He smelled the back of his hand. "Jesus," he said. "When you come home, we have something to do."

I was not so young as to be ignorant of what was going on. I had a friend, Cooper Fennimore, whose house

I slept over at whenever possible because his father had a drawerful of Penthouse. The first time, we had stolen one and flipped it open to a picture of a woman's massive red nails, and a belt of ammo under them, and a thick brown bush under that. Within the bush were two lips like you could make by lacing fingers with a friend and spreading them open, but thicker, like your friend had meaty fingers. When it came to dogs, however, I wasn't sure about the situation. I didn't consult Cooper or anyone else at school. I didn't want to talk about the look of my faithful and stupid dog's vagina.

When I came home that afternoon, the dog was waiting at the door for me, as she always did. She jumped up on me in a happy and normal way. I made Nestle Quik and ate dry Cheerios and fed them to her while watching Power Rangers. My father came home and thumped his briefcase on the hall floor. This triggered something in Tam, and she mounted the briefcase.

My father kicked her off, picked up the briefcase by the sides and smelled the top of it. "Son of a bitch," he said. "Sam, come upstairs and bring the dog."

When I got upstairs he was in the bathroom with his sleeves rolled up and three q-tips in one hand. "This isn't going to be the greatest," he said.

I thought he was going to stab her in the vagina, or at least stuff her up. I said, "Dad" in that embarrassing way that disappoints both father and son.

"Do you want her in bed with you like this? Is there something going on here? I know you take a lot of naps together."

"No."

"Do you want that smell in your face?" Here he turned Tam around, panting and generally curious, so that little meat flower was winking in my face. It smelled like trash from my parent's bathroom wastebasket, which was a foot or two away from me, combined with the smell of a used Bandaid. "Do you want to wake up to that?"

9

"No."

"Then hold her tight. She's going to squirm a little." He spun Tam back around and steadied her backside with one hand. The other held one q-tip, poised like he was going to gut her. She licked my face. "That a girl." He said. "That a girl."

When he first started going at it, Tam wrestled in discomfort. I thought he was hurting her. This was my dog, and I wanted it to stop, but I didn't say anything. My dad had a look on his face like he was staring at a gutter full of leaves.

"Attagirl," My father said. "Happens to the best of us. Attagirl, get it out of your system."

Then Tam's tempo changed, got more regular and more insistent. She got the same look that my father had, focused but not entirely sold on the proceedings. Her front legs were locked in place. Her back was arched, like an angry cat's. She pumped away, and my father took it. I didn't know where to look. I certainly didn't want to look at my father, and I most certainly did not want to look at Tam. I also didn't want to admit my displeasure, get all sissied out like I had before, so I stared at her chest. It had a furry star of white squarely in the center, a proud thing.

She bucked a little more determinedly, almost coming out of my grip, then paused with her back at full arch. She thumped twice more at my father, like she was trying to bite him with her butt. Then she relaxed, panted a little, and licked my hand.

"All good? There you go, shit for brains," He patted her rump and threw the q-tip into the wastebasket. He stood with his hands in front of him, held up with the palms towards his chest. Tam trotted out the room and down the stairs. "Let's wash up."

He washed in his sink, and I washed in my mom's, though my hands hadn't really been part of the action. We scrubbed our hands without speaking, just like we did when I was younger and he had to take me to the bath-

11

room in restaurants.

"Well that puts you off your dinner, huh? How much homework do you have, lots? No? Did it at school? Alright, we going to watch Friends tonight?" It was Thursday, and my father and I were both deeply invested in the Ross and Rachel romance. We didn't go out for ice cream that night, but we did pretty soon after, and the both of us got mocha frappes.

two poems

Daniel Robbins

in lieu of writing

I take delight in so many things: rearranging the bookshelves,
Jimmy Giuffre on vinyl, some days even chores I give myself
like washing pollen from the car, wiping dust from the ceiling fan
and, since it is the final days of fall, some afternoons I pick
stones from the land where I will make a garden next year.
But tonight, I not-write by searching for the history of my
family name, and I do it ill-prepared, without my elders to
guide me through the fog of my kin: those spoken of rarely
and those spoken of none and those about which no one knows.
Before my second cigarette I am out of answers, so I abandon
fact, abandon memory, and instead I decide to trace my lineage
only by hunch, by the names of the Robbins men that sound
sturdy and wagoned like Obadiah or Solomon, Milton and Moses,
Orion, men from the desert of Tennessee who had many children
and placed little allegories within them: firstborn Thankful, baby
Consider, the only child Obediance who died before age 10 among
the Nixburg trees. But when I came to know my past for certain,
how I now know what is true, was found by looking at the names
of women they loved—sounds of phonetic desire on my tongue
that I fall in love with also: Althea; Lovey West; Virginia and
Sarah Adeline; Deliverance; Delila; Permelia and Adelia and yes,
Absolom; and now I understand where I've gone wrong, the secret
of all failed coupling hiding in these names: the consonant grunts
and sibilant teases—Tasha and Shelby and Shelly—the flighty
affricates of Jenny and Julie and the delicate Cheree; and how,
I ask myself, could I have not seen the fate of palindromic Anna,
for whom my love reads the same both ways in time—little body

15

of passion I once never knew. This is the wisdom my ancestors
have left for me, and to honor their good names I tell them, in
the quiet of night: ghosts of my precursors, your deaths are not
forgotten; next time I love, it will be built on the sound of it;
it will be for a woman of Adamic descent, postscript of Eve who
will be named a motion and song, a finger to the lip, the voice
unformed humming a melody that all lives before me can hum too.
Make this my epitaph and bury me deep—no, burn the body,
but place a stone in the earth all the same.

The Scientific American on the Uses of Air in the Age of Reason

is the title of a pamphlet I found folded
inside a library book I never read about
the Falklands War, and it is this day's
best thing—not because of the tales
it holds of those perilous first ballooners,
nor of the Byzantine size of the pipe organ
built for a palace in Constantinople, and
not even for its explication of the curves
sculpted into lavish Arabian architecture,
meant to keep the cool air flowing.
No, what made this gentile paper
transcend its ephemeral tribe was words
some previous reader had written upon it,
over an image of the first recorded
parachute jump (1783), placed so appropriately
as if by myself from a previous life,
perhaps then also sitting at a window,
drinking coffee, waiting out a rainstorm
and love for a ghost, secretly hoping
neither passes. How much I wish
something—some document, some note,
some glyph on a cave wall in a distant,
even mythical, land—would tell me secrets
of this prior life, teach me what sustained
whomever had come before in this world
and, in the heavy light of all the heart's things,
saw the necessity to write *help me*, in blue ink,
coming from the mouth of that first parachutist,
pioneer of falling. What happened to you,
guardian—prologue of this life who tried

to unwrite history and save some foolish
footnoted man descending to earth by
writing into time a voice calling out to God
or anyone who will listen, then added
speed lines to emphasize the urgency?

Sy Hoahwah

Breaking In

I began a road trip to Los Angeles on New Year's Eve 2010 to do a few poetry readings. It was my first attempt at promoting *Velroy and the Madischie Mafia* (West End Press 2009), my first full-length collection. During the first week of the new year my 3-day, California reading tour was to start out in Santa Ana, CA and end up in L.A. I was going to headline with a friend who also had a book out. It was my first time to do anything like this as a published poet with a book, and it was my first time in California. It was my first time to celebrate a victory in a long time. So along the way I made a couple of stops.

Starting out from Little Rock, AR, I picked up my nephew and younger sister. At that time, my nephew Payton was an undergraduate at the University of Central Arkansas, majoring in English with an emphasis in creative writing. My little sister Lindsay was at the crossroads of deciding what to do about college, career, and life. In other words, she was just sitting at home playing online games on her computer all day, or sketching another idea for an anime comic book. Then there was me, the older brother, the uncle, the one who always seems to be pedaling in the mud—according to the older family members. But for all of us, it was our first true road trip together, all of us now as adults.

We stopped off in Fayetteville the first night, the home of the University of Arkansas where I got my M.F.A. in creative writing a few years earlier. I really can't say if all my learning came from the classes and instructors. I can't remember the classes I took, nor any godly advice from

the instructor/poet. Most of it came from very few fellow students who were also there trying to learn something they didn't already know about poetry. Through all the poetry workshops, literature courses, and thesis hours, I managed to keep my head and concept of self-preservation intact, and to form friendships with some of the most remarkable individuals I had met in a really long time. These friendships today are bonds that are detrimental to me, and that I will keep for the rest of my life.

So there we are at about 5:30 pm, at the doorstep of my best friend poetry combat sibling, Chris Pappas, and I am meeting his wife Rebecca for the first time. We are supposed to all head to L.A. together the next morning. About 5:40 pm we start celebrating New Year's Eve, the new year, and the publication of my first book of poetry which had come out that September. It is a fabulous night of seeing old friends, and for the first time to see my little sister get drunk on Yellow Tail wine, and vomit in the little bathroom sink that was already stopped up. I have the pleasure to finally sit down and visit with Chris's wife Rebecca. It is an introduction which has been waiting to happen for about a year plus. Chris was right; she is fearless.

The next afternoon, after much debate about travel plans and deliberate attempts at getting coordinated, we finally say our goodbyes.

Our next stop is Lawton, Oklahoma. We have to make it to New Year's Comanche Powwow that night and meet up with my uncle. All the way out to New Mexico it is like this, we make several stops to visit friends and extended family. The day before the first scheduled reading we finally make it to the California border in the afternoon. I remember this because I make sure to show the border patrol both my driver's license and tribal I.D. card. I don't want any confusion about my nationality.

When we get into Barstow, I call my host to tell him we are getting somewhat close. Now this host is nice

enough to put us up for the few days we are going to be out there, even though I have never met the guy before in my life.

Let me explain what little back history I have with this individual, at this point. He is the host of an online blog radio program based out of L.A. When *Velroy* was published his radio show was one of the first interviews I did to promote the book. After the interview, he told me that he actually enjoyed the book and thought Los Angeles would be a great place for me to start on a reading tour. I contacted him a week or so later and agreed to come out. I worked it out with my friend, who would be driving in from San Diego for us to read together at these venues. We support each other's books as we can. The host was in love with the idea, and promised us good venues where we would be headliners. There would even be a couple of readings on the Sunset Strip. He assured me that he could put me up at his place, along with my nephew and sister. Apparently his cousin had a vacant furnished home where we could stay. I was really psyched about the idea too, at that point. Because for me to do a reading tour, I would have to pay for everything myself (gas, hotel, and food). My publisher could only afford to send me a single small shipment of books as payment for publication rights. So anything involving readings comes out of my pocket, and I try to make the money back out of the books I personally sell at readings.

So there we are in my Saturn *LE* just leaving the outskirts of Barstow, and I call our host. I tell him where we are, and he advises me to call him back when we get to San Bernardino. I do.

After that, from San Bernardino to North Hollywood, the guy calls my cell phone every 15 minutes to get a status report. During the status reports I get the directions to his residence, which is located off Van Nuys Ave. Thank god for the GPS system on cell phones. The host tells us once we pull up on his street, he will meet us

in this parking lot. So we get there and park in this vacant parking lot with no street lights. In the shadows lurks the host.

The only contact I have had with this person is by cell phone. By his voice, I had pictured him a bit of a hipsterish, tofu-eating, Latino, up and coming poet in his mid to late twenties who had an edge, as well as connections, due to his online radio show.

Out of the dark and into the headlights of my car, here comes a 45 year old, short, scruffy, truck-driver looking guy—wearing thick lensed glasses in frames that had to be at least fifteen years old. His teeth are dark brown from drinking $20 pots of black coffee all his adult life at cafes tucked neatly in the corners of the L.A. poetry scene. Despite the initial shock of appearances (me being a 6'4, 300 lb Comanche man who writes poetry), I thought we would bump fists and greet each other as if comrades-in-arms. But no, the only greeting we get is, "Follow me…."

So I leave my car in this vacant lot. After passing a couple of burnt-out houses and the burnt wire frame of a couch sitting on the sidewalk, we get to our "furnished place to stay." But to actually get to the entrance we have to navigate down this ill-lit driveway. It is a 25 yard long labyrinth of 8 ft. walls, stacked cinder blocks, and broken down RVs. Three to be exact. We enter the residence; it is a garage—where our host lives. Inside is his bed, which is the top part of a children's bunk bed. Underneath the bed, hang his clothes. And he has a love seat and a small bed stand with a TV on it. The linoleum floor is covered with trash and dirty clothes. But in one corner of the garage there are a couple of shelves hung on the wall. Neatly placed on the shelves in alphabetical order are books of poetry—classical, modern, and contemporary. Lying in the loveseat and watching TV is the host's girlfriend, who is in a creative writing program somewhere in the greater central California area.

This is where the host is planning for us to stay.

This is the cousin's vacant furnished residence. The host insists that my sister, nephew and myself, all three of us, sleep in his bunk bed. As I mentioned earlier, I am a big guy; my nephew is about the same size as me. The two of us alone could not fit in that child bed. The host is well pleased by this arrangement, but his girlfriend is not. She wants to sleep with me and my nephew while her boyfriend sleeps on the floor with my sister. My group immediately suggests other arrangements, like—we will sleep on the floor. Well the host has another idea.

He suggests another room that is in the house next door which is apparently on the same property. So we follow him through a series of doorways and small corridors and finally reach the outside of the garage and walk across this pathway into the next house. Now this house is empty except for this old ratty couch that is propped up against the wall because it has only two legs diagonal from each other. Although there are no locks on the doors, "it is safe." The host says my sister can sleep here and we (nephew and me) can sleep next door on the floor underneath the host and his girlfriend. As he is suggesting this, a thin man with dishwater blond hair and a thin mustache suddenly appears from the back of this vacant house and states that "a lot of hookers have slept on this couch." He is the host's cousin. He disappears to the back of the house again, from where he came.

After looking at the fight or flight faces on my nephew and sister, I tell the host that we do not want to put him out, and that for tonight we will just get a hotel room. We walk back to the garage where his bed is, still trying to convince this guy that we will be fine with a hotel room. All of us are exhausted at this point for we have driven all day and night, and just want to collapse somewhere without the fear of some stranger jumping us violently or sexually. At one point, I just tell him to literally point to the direction where there are some hotels, and we will be on our way. He insists on picking out the hotel

for us. He gets on his "laptop," which actually is an internet keyboard. Host and girlfriend argue about the failure of sleeping arrangements and which hotels are cheap. So after fifteen minutes of haggling with this guy about what hotels to stay at, we pick one, and from nowhere appears the cousin again and agrees on the hotel suggestion: "You might want to stay there because there are a lot of hookers that hang out there." Once again he disappears into the next room. So we go back and pick a different hotel.

The host and girlfriend suggest we follow them in our car to the hotel. Sounds like a good idea, so we navigate back through the cinder block corridors and broken down RVs to the sidewalk. And as we turn down the sidewalk the same cousin comes pulling up in a minivan with a middle-aged black woman in the passenger side.

We finally get to the hotel; it is very old. Keys are still being used instead of access cards. Plus the manager doesn't speak English and has trouble swiping my sister's credit card. I only work on a cash basis. So we decide to go across the street to the Holiday Inn. As I walk back to get into the car, the host and girlfriend are on the hood of my car making out. I know her pants are about to come off. Goddamn!

Once we get into our hotel room with contemporary accessories and access cards, and give the host and girlfriend the brush off, I make the decision that we are going back home tomorrow night. Our options of places to stay are slim. I don't know anybody in L.A. except my friend John, but he is M.I.A. We had only enough money for food, and that was spent up in the hotel charge. There is barely enough money to make it back to Oklahoma. Hopefully with the money we have and with the money I will make from book sells, we will make it. It's like *Grapes of Wrath* in reverse for us.

The next morning the host insists that we meet him and girlfriend for breakfast, and from there they will show us around. Breakfast is at this trendy little greasy

spoon (if a greasy spoon can be trendy), where they serve hubcap-sized pancakes. As we walk in, of course it is crowded, with waiters, waitresses, and customers dressed ultra hipsterish. They seem ever-so-ready to audition at the drop of the word. We are seated at the back of the establishment in a room with no windows, just the door with a single window pane in it, and situated close to the bathrooms. We get the pancakes and three rounds of $20 pots of black coffee. Although the host took us out for breakfast, we end up paying for ourselves.

The host had promised to show us around. Well the night before, after we decided to cut this trip short, we also decided that we would visit at least one place in L.A. before we left. We all picked Venice Beach. So I tell the host that we want to go to Venice Beach. It is about 12:30 pm at this point, and we are nowhere near the beach.

Once I got into the L.A. metro area, I immediately learned that it takes forever to get anywhere because of the damn population in the way. Before we can go to the beach the host wants to take me to this bookstore owned by one of his friends. I agree to it and follow him and girlfriend to the bookstore. It takes us forever to find the place. We drive around in circles for two hours. He says he knows where he is going, and that we are close to the beach. We finally get there and have to go around the block five times in order to get a parking spot; then, of course, the book store is closed. I am cool with this, and we finally go to the beach. I have to pay for them to park because they have no cash. That's fine because we are finally at Venice Beach.

Even though Venice Beach is definitely toned down these days and not as colorful as it once was, it is still good to be here, to walk and see the Pacific Ocean for the first time, and Malibu, just a rocket launch away. The host finally does something cool: he takes me to this bookstore that is on the beach, and I am able to leave a couple of books there on consignment. I could care less

if they sell. For me it is a monumental "to do" to leave a copy of my first book at Venice Beach where Jim Morrison roamed as he copied down in his journals the ideas for songs that made up most of the first album of The Doors.

The rest of the afternoon is spent trying to get to Santa Ana for the reading. The reading is scheduled for 7:00 pm. We leave the beach around 4:40. First I have to take a wicked piss as does everyone else. So we stop at one gas station on our way out of L.A., with no bathroom. The host says he knows of a nearby coffee shop, so we go there and wait in line for the bathroom. Then the host wants some coffee. But I really need to get on the road because I promised to meet my friend (with whom I am reading), early before the show so we can visit and get dinner.

So here we are in line getting more coffee. I have finally had enough and tell the host that we were taking off to Santa Ana and that we know the way. That is not good enough. He wants to show us where to go on his "laptop" even though I told him I have GPS on my cell phone. Then he Google maps it for us anyway. But then his "laptop" runs out of battery. Next he wants us to follow him all the way back to his house so he can get his power cord for the "laptop." I finally say,"Fuck it, we are taking off." My crew walks out the door and finally leaves the host and girlfriend. We literally jump into the car and blaze to Santa Ana, going over South Central L.A.—Compton and Crenshaw. By the time we get to the bar where we are to read, my friend is already there scoping the place out.

There is something to be said when you drive 2,000 miles to do a reading that you think you are head-lining only to find out that the reading that was suppos-edly set-up for you and your friend exclusively, is really an open-mic night at a second rate sandwich shop and bar. In other words, I could be psychopathic Joe Blow who just walked off the street and signed up for a reading spot, in which I might read from a collection of poems composed on my forearm with a sharpened butter knife, and read

them off my bloody arm. My friend and I are really disappointed. Come to find out, all these so-called headlining venues are open-mic nights. Fuck this! All day I felt guilty that we had already decided to leave after the reading, ditching the host and the gigs to go back home, due to our lack of funds.

My friend and I go ahead and sign up to read for the night. Do I sell any books? Hell no! The crowd is mostly made up of people over the age of 50, or young single families who brought their kids for the discount special the sandwich shop offers on this particular night. The host and girlfriend show up during my friend's reading. They sit down with us. The girlfriend asks me if we could give the host a ride back because she has to go study. I don't answer.

I finish my reading set after waiting through five horrific readings (one was an upper-class 40-ish chick with daddy's girl problems, the father being dead for 20 years; another one was a young man with one long hacky poem about the staples in the spine of a particular chapbook he read the week before). The host is going to read now. Right before he goes on, I tell him that we are going with my friend back to San Diego to spend the night and see the sites the next day. It wouldn't be until 4 a.m. in the morning, as we are getting close to Grants, New Mexico, that I call him and leave a message that we are heading back home. So as he reads, we slip out, and immediately throw my box of books in the trunk and get the hell out of there. For I have the fear that at any moment the host may lay the hammer down on us as we are getting into the car and ask for a ride back to his place—and ask us to stay.

As my nephew accesses the GPS on his cell phone, I direct the car out of L.A. and into the darkness of the hinterlands. We tear through the blackness of a January desert night getting out of California. Seeing the last light of California fade out, I realize that being a poet sucks.

USPOCO BOOKS is a division of us poetry company, a constantly touring personal service corp. formed by Chris and Rebecca Pappas on April 1st, 2009 in Fayetteville, AR. *The Road To Nowhere Tour* began on May 29, 2009.

Founded with a group of professors, students and local artists frustrated by the seeming impossibility of useful learning while confined in competing institutional roles, the first members of us poetry company organized to push for curriculum reform at The University of Arkansas in some fairly innovative ways.

The troupe demonstrated what it saw as the new educational model, by writing plays to learn English composition, by using collaborative methods for creating poetry and short fiction to be performed or published on any corner of campus, and by becoming active in a campus movement for general curriculum reform. Some of the students involved went on to found art-centered student groups and literary journals.

Over three years of touring, performing, and teaching, us poetry company has developed an improvisational teaching style for improvisational minds; we are now implementing this new style and new curriculum in community based educational programs, as well as academic based programs.

us poetry company offers teacher enrichment training, business writing courses, camps, and classes in the arts, as well as personalized poetry instruction for all ages.

ManuFactured Artists is a grass roots community of writers working for writers. Email the editors at **uspocobooks@gmail.com** for more info. Or visit us at **uspoco.com** and **ManuFacturedArtists.com**.

www.ingramcontent.com/pod-product-compliance
Lightning Source LLC
Chambersburg PA
CBHW072047170626
46811CB00008B/3196